SECOND EDITION

Storybook 4

The Octopus Book

by Sue Dickson

Illustrations by Norma Portadino, Jean Hamilton, Chip Neville and Kerstin Upmeyer

Printed in the United States of America

Copyright © 1998 Sue Dickson
International Learning Systems of North America, Inc.
St. Petersburg, FL 33716

ISBN: 1-56704-514-6 (Volume 4)

C D E F G H I J K L M N—CJK—05 04 03 02 01 99

ŏ

Vocabulary of 32 Words

dot

hop

hog

got

log

hot

Mom

rob

box

doll

not

ox

cot

stop

lot

Todd

pot

jog

tom-tom

dog

lock

clock

rock

fox

top

from

spot

blocks

odd

sock

pop

on

Words with
letters that
steal another
letter's sound are

RULE
BREAKERS

was
(wŭz)

to

..REVIEW VOCABULARY.

sat	Pep	him
red	his	got
Sis	pop	wet
on	Pam	the
had	left	miss
bed	will	doll
is	pot	map
Mom	Dad	less
cat	help	Jill
pen	Jim	hop
not	log	as
kiss	have	yell
a	yet	give

4

.....ă.....ĕ.....ĭ.....and...ŏ

glad	past	ten
pet	gets	Biff
pig	in	to
cot	top	gas
was	cap	bent
went	end	will
big	dip	hot
lot	rob	has
wag	tan	mess
beg	Todd	milk
fit	fill	stop
dog	hog	fat
	pass	men

Teacher,
"Gus" is hiding in this book.
You may want to ask students
to find Gus.

Kim,

Jill

**and
Pep**

Jill has a doll.

Jill's doll is Kim.

Kim has on a red hat.

It has a pom-pom on top.

Kim has on big red dots.

8

Jill set Kim on the doll bed.

Pep ran to get Kim.

Pep got Kim !

Pep held Kim and ran fast.

A dog can rob a doll bed.

10

Pep ran fast and
did not stop.

Pep ran to the logs.

A big pot was on the logs.

Pep hid Kim in the big pot.
Pep ran as fast as a fox !

Jill went to get Kim.

Kim was not in bed !

A red hat was on
the bed, not Kim !

13

Jill ran to Mom.
"Mom, Mom !
I had Kim in bed.
Kim's red hat is in bed,
not Kim !"

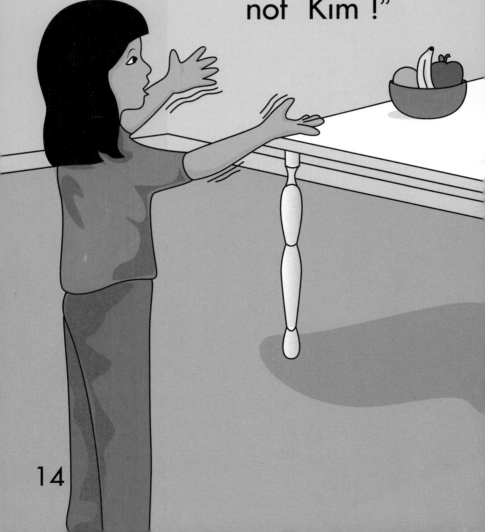

"Ask Todd.
Todd has a
box, and it
has a lot
in it."

15

Jill ran to Todd.

"Kim is not in bed !"

Did Todd have Kim ?

Todd had a man.

Todd had a hen.

Todd did not have Kim.

Todd had a top.

Todd had a tom-tom.

Todd had ten blocks.

Todd did not have Kim.

Todd had a bat.

Todd had a lock, and
Todd had an odd sock.

Todd did not have Kim.

Todd has a big rock.

It has a red spot on it.

Todd has a van.

Todd did not have Kim.

Todd has a man.

The man can jog.

Todd did not have Kim.

21

Todd had a jet
and a clock.

Todd had a hog
and an ox.

Todd did not have Kim.

22

Kim was not in the box.

Pep ran to Jill and Todd.

Wag, wag, wag, went Pep.

Pep had a big red dot !

Pep has Kim's big red dot !
Yet Pep did not have Kim.

"Get Kim !"
    Jill did yell.

"Get Kim !

Pep is a bad dog !"

"Get Kim, Pep !"

Pep ran fast as a fox.

Pep ran to the big pot

26   on the log.

A dog can hop on the log.

Pep got the doll
from the pot.

At last, Jill has Kim !
Jill is glad.

28   Pep is not a bad dog.

Pep can not have Kim.

Pep can pick from
   Todd's box.

Will Pep pick the top ?

Pep will pick Todd's hog.

Todd is glad.

Pep is glad.

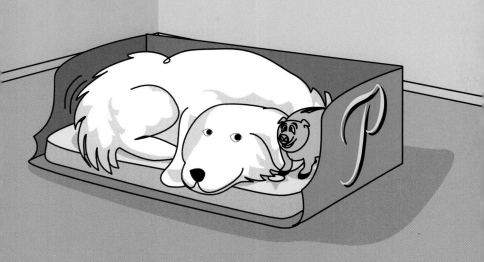

Pep got on his cot.

At last, Pep can rest,
and Pep's hog can rest
on his cot.

Pep can have a nap.

31

Mom will let Jill
and Todd yell
and hop !

The End